Table of Contents

Teacher Tips

Encourage Topic Interest

Help children develop an understanding and appreciation of different outdoor education concepts by providing an area in the classroom to display topic-related non-fiction books, pictures, collections, and artifacts as a springboard for learning.

What I Think I Know/What I Would Like to Know Activity

Introduce each outdoor education concept by asking children what they think they know about the topic, and what they would like to know about the topic. Complete this activity as a whole-group brainstorming session, in cooperative small groups, or independently. Once children have had a chance to complete the questions, combine the information to create a class chart for display. Throughout the study, periodically update children's progress in accomplishing their goal of what they want to know, and validate what they think they know.

Vocabulary List

Keep track of new and content-related vocabulary on chart paper for children's reference. Encourage children to add words to the list. Classify the word list into the categories of nouns, verbs, and adjectives. In addition, have children create their own dictionaries as part of their learning logs.

Learning Logs

Keeping a learning log is an effective way for children to organize thoughts and ideas about the outdoor education concepts presented and examined. Children's learning logs also provide insight on what follow-up activities are needed to review and to clarify concepts learned. Learning logs can include the following types of entries:

- Teacher prompts
- Personal reflections
- Questions that arise
- Connections discovered
- Labelled diagrams and pictures
- Definitions for new vocabulary

Outdoor Education

What is Outdoor Education?

Outdoor education engages children in authentic, real-world experiences outside of the classroom walls. This experience fosters a healthy respect for nature and inspires children to become environmental advocates and problem -solvers for the future.

Creating an outdoor classroom provides children with space to actively and freely engage with the environment, explore curiosities and gain knowledge in a meaningful way. Most importantly, children gather the first-hand experience of the interconnectedness of humans, animals, and plants while having direct contact with weather and seasons.

Benefits for Children

- Inspires a healthy and active lifestyle by freely moving in the outdoors
- Fosters interest in STEM activities and the environment by connecting with nature
- Increases motivation for learning as children' curiosity about the workings of the natural environment drives their pursuit of knowledge
- Provides enriched opportunities for children to explore, discover and problem solve with peers
- Boost independence and confidence in children as they learn how to direct their learning through outdoor inquiries
- Builds stewardship skills and an appreciation for the environment
- Decreases stress as children are in a natural setting and encourage mindfulness
- Improves retention of knowledge as authentic, meaningful hands-on learning helps children to retain knowledge weather and seasons

Developing an Outdoor Learning Program

Find a Location

Look for an outdoor setting easily accessible all year-round that will allow children to interact with a variety of natural elements (various trees, plants, soil, grass, garden, mulch, gravel, etc.) This can be a designated area of the school field, a courtyard or a nearby park.

Design Boundaries

Once you have an ideal location, mark clear boundaries in this setting with fencing or pylons. Review boundaries with children frequently. For example, children know to stay within a fenced area, or not to go past a specific tree, don't go near play equipment, etc.

Find Support

Enlist the school administrator, fellow teachers, older children, parents and community partners to help develop your outdoor education program. Remember help can come in many forms, from applying for government grants, donation of materials, co-planning lessons or volunteer gardeners, working as a team is very important. The more people who believe in the program, the more it will be able to grow over time.

Commit to a Schedule

Designate a spot in your timetable to have regular outdoor education time (ideally once a day, or week) that can be committed to throughout the year.

Start Small

Begin by introducing your children to the environment. Establish routines, let them explore and play freely before entering lessons. After children begin to feel more comfortable in the outdoor classroom, you can introduce learning tasks.

Outdoor Classroom Storage and Supplies

Keep materials dedicated to outdoor learning organized, and accessible. Here are some suggestions for storage and materials to keep on hand.

Storage Ideas

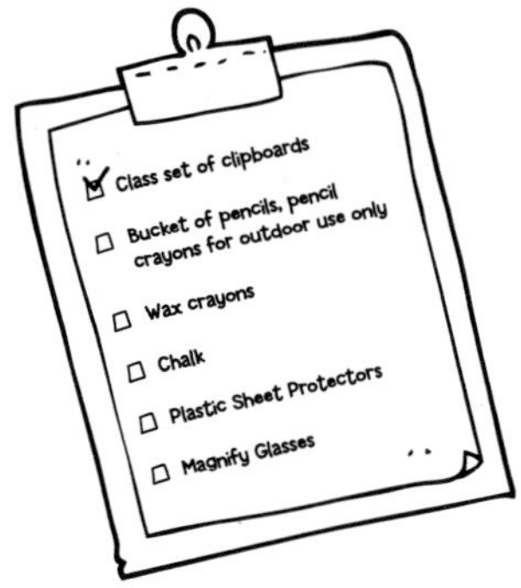

Shed

This allows outdoor materials to stay outdoors.
Organize the shed with labels and shelves.

Mobile Cart

An advantage of a mobile cart is that it can be easily transported in and out of the classroom. Load with clipboards, pencils and outdoor materials needed for the lesson.

Wagon

Transport materials and supplies quickly and easily. Wagons are easy to load, unload and change contents frequently. Wagons can be stored inside or outside.

Supplies

These outdoor education supplies are ideal for facilitating outdoor activities.

- Class set of clipboards
- Bucket of pencils, pencil crayons for outdoor use only
- Waxe crayons
- Chalk
- Plastic Sheet Protectors
- Magnify Glasses
- Pylons
- Garden stakes for labelling
- Strong string
- Hula Hoops
- Binders with sheet protectors to store children work in one place
- Pinnies for younger children to ensure visibility of their whereabouts
- Tarp to use as an outdoor carpet or mat
- Clear plastic bags or brown paper bags to collect natural items
- Small jars to collect living things or soil samples
- A whistle for command attention and or emergencies

Outdoor Classroom Play-Based Centres

Play-based centres allow children to take charge of their learning, make choices and explore possibilities in a safe setting. This is an ideal way to engage younger children in a variety of tasks providing abundant learning opportunities through interactions with the natural environment and sharing ideas with their peers. It also allows the educator to work one on one or with small groups of children while the rest of the class engages in meaningful play.

Keeping Organized

Keep materials for individual centres in separate bins so that the activity is easily accessible. Also, make sure there are enough materials for each child, along with a sample of what is expected if possible. Furthermore:

- Introduce and explain the expectation of each learning centre for children.
- Model and reinforce skills needed to complete an art activity.

Establishing Routines

Establish clear expectations and responsibilities of children while at each centre and the number of children allowed per centre. Also, make sure children are involved in cleanup and know where to put away materials. The educator may wish to ring a bell, play music, blow a whistle to signal when it is time to move to a different centre or to clean up.

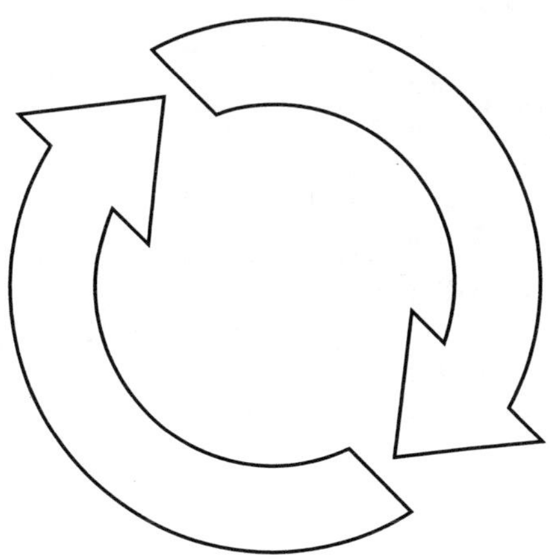

Outdoor Play-Based Centres

Centre Ideas	Autumn Materials	Winter Materials	Spring Materials	Summer Materials
Nature Exploration	• tree cookies • dry leaves • acorns • twigs	• pinecones • pine branches • logs • salt	• rocks • seed pods • sticks • pebbles	• sea glass • dried flowers • shells • dandelions
Gross Motor	• hula hoops • walking stilts • wagons	• sleds • sliding carpets • shovels	• scooters • wheel barrows • car tires	• kites • frisbees • ribbon sticks
Dramatic Play	**Kitchen Drama Centre** • pots • pans • wooden spoons • muffin tins • plastic plates • plastic cups • plastic utensils	**Theatre Drama Centre** • make puppets with natural materials • build theatre seats	**Campsite Drama Centre** • set up a tent • build a pretend fire • build fishing rods	**Farm Drama Centre** • egg cartons • milking buckets • wheel barrow • wagon • gardening tools
Weaving Wall Centre	• provide string to make a spider web	• decorate the weaving wall by hanging holiday decorations	• create a quilt using long pieces of fabric	• create a giant dream catcher
Building Centre	• wooden planks • wooden blocks • tree stumps • logs	• snow brick building • shovels • rolling snow boulders	• tarp • ropes • eaves troughs • plastic pipes	• pool noodle bits • pool noodles • hula hoop huts
Sensory Centre	• corn kernels • beans • sunflower seeds • pumpkin guts • cranberries • wind chimes	• sound wall • sound jars • jingle bells • coloured ice • balloon ice chunks • cinnamon sticks	• dyed rice • rain sticks • clay • seeds • mud • mulch	• water wall • bubbles • moon sand • fresh herbs • dyed chickpeas • berries

Outdoor Warm Up Activities

Warm up activities for the outdoor classroom provide exciting and stimulating ways to begin your class. These activities involve minimal materials and are child directed. Further, they can be completed all year round. Educators are encouraged to implement these activities multiple times throughout the school term. This will provide children with the opportunity to demonstrate their growth and for teachers to assess their progress.

While children are busy completing their tasks, educators may use this time to set up centres, materials, and experiments in the outdoor classroom.

Establishing routines for each activity is essential, this way children can take charge of their learning and complete the tasks with independence and confidence.

Teacher Tips

- Tie pencils to clipboards with string.
- Review appropriate "on task" behaviour.
- Take pictures of children demonstrating "on task" behavior and share them with the class to show what routines should "look like".
- Teach children how to correctly put away materials.
- Assign a class leader or monitor to be responsible of specific frequently used items (i.e. clipboard collector, pencil sharpener, magnify glass monitor).
- Have a class set up clipboards in an accessible/portable place.

Animal Moves

Discuss with children how different animals move in different ways. Let children know that they are going try moving like different animals. As each animal is called along with a type of movement, have children imitate the movement. Allow children to imitate each animal movement for at least 15 seconds. You may wish to have children brainstorm additional animals and their movements. Here are some ideas to start:

- **Bird** (flap your arms)
- **Crab** (sit with your hands on the floor behind you, use your feet to lift your body, walk backward on your hands and feet)
- **Duck** (fold arms in, bend down, and waddle)
- **Elephant** (stomp feet and swing arm in front like an elephant's trunk)
- **Frog** (squat down, put your hands on the floor, and jump up and down)
- **Giraffe** (walk while trying to stretch your neck up high)
- **Groundhog** (walk on your knees and simulate pushing away dirt)
- **Horse** (gallop)
- **Hummingbird** (arms rotating forward, then backward)
- **Kangaroo** (long jumps)

- **Lion** (walk with both hands and feet on the floor)
- **Monkey** (swing your arms on the spot as if climbing a tree, and make monkey faces)
- **Peacock** (strut with your hands fluttering behind your back and your head held high)
- **Penguin** (waddle without bending your legs and keeps hands to the sides)
- **Rabbit** (hop)
- **Snake** (slither like a snake by pushing yourself along on your tummy)
- **Turtle** (crawl very slowly on your hands and knees)
- **Worm** (wiggle whole body)

Variation—Animal Relay Race: Children will not only get great exercise, but they will also learn the importance of cooperation and working toward a common goal. Divide children into 4 to 6 teams. Assign each child a different animal movement for their part of the relay. Each child moves as their animal from the starting line to a designated turning point and back. The first team to have all children finish wins.

Tag Games

Tag games are good physical activities because they create a great deal of excitement and interest among the players. Tag games also increase the heart rate and breathing rate, develop gross motor skills and coordination, and exercise all the muscles of the body. Because tag games are generally played outdoors, participants also benefit from plenty of fresh air and sunshine. Other benefits include increased attention span, better performance in school, reduced risk of obesity and its related illnesses, and increased confidence and sportsmanship. Whether these games are played at school or at home with friends, tag games have a magnetic quality that makes children—and adults!—want to participate.

Animal Tag

1. Choose one player to be "It" and choose the first animal for all players to imitate.
2. Tell players they will play a tag game in which they must move like different animals, while trying to avoid being tagged. Explain that this game is very fast-paced and that, every 20 seconds, you will choose a new player to be It and give them a different animal to imitate.
3. If a player does not move like the designated animal, they must step out until the next round begins.
4. Tagged players must remain frozen in place, but can be unfrozen when touched by a fellow player.
5. After 20 seconds or so, choose a new player as It and give players a new animal to imitate. Remind players to move like the newest animal. You can also help with clues about how to move, such as "jump like a kangaroo," "swing your arm like an elephant's trunk," or "swish your tail like a lion."
6. Make sure that every player has a chance to be It.

Tag Games

Caterpillar Tag

1. Choose a player to be "It."
2. Explain that when a player is tagged, that player must hold onto the shoulders of the player who is It. The players move around the room together, tagging other players. Every player who is tagged joins the end of the caterpillar and holds onto the shoulders of the player in front of them.
3. Players in the caterpillar can all tag other players, as long as they keep one hand holding onto the player ahead of them.
4. The game ends when all of the players have joined the caterpillar.

Spider and Flies Tag

1. Choose one player to be the Spider. The rest of the players will be Flies.
2. Every Fly the Spider tags becomes part of the Spider's web. Flies that are tagged must hold hands with the Spider and with each other to form a long chain. These Flies work together with the Spider to catch other Flies, but only the Flies on the ends of the chain can tag other players.
3. Players can run under the arms of the Flies to avoid being caught. The last remaining player becomes the next Spider.

Catch-a-Rainbow Tag

1. Set up two lines about 20 metres apart.
2. Choose one player to be the Rainbow Catcher who will stand in the middle between the two lines.
3. Tell players they will be assigned a colour of the rainbow—red, orange, yellow, green, blue, purple. Whisper a different colour to each player so the Rainbow Catcher does not hear it.
4. After the colours are assigned, the Rainbow Catcher calls out a colour. The players who have that colour run to the other line, trying not to get tagged.
5. When the Rainbow Catcher tags a player, that player goes to the middle to help tag other players.
6. Instead of calling an individual colour, the Rainbow Catcher can sometimes call "Rainbow!" so all players have to run at once.
7. The last player left becomes the next Rainbow Catcher.

Parachute Games

Parachute games are moderate physical activities that have an exciting and sometimes calming effect on participants. The billowing, graceful beauty of the parachute and the rustle of the fabric often induce feelings of amazement and awe. Parachute games encourage cooperation among participants and are a good base for noncompetitive play activities. Parachute games strengthen the muscles in the shoulders, upper arms, and hands, and help participants develop perceptual skills and rhythm. These high-interest games are particularly fun to play outdoors on a warm, sunny day.

Ocean Waves

Have all players grip the edges of the parachute on the ground, and shake it up and down with small movements. Pretend you are making ocean waves, sand dunes, a pizza with bubbling cheese, etc.

Balancing Act

Instruct all players to hold onto the edges of the parachute tightly. All at once, have everyone lean back while still holding onto the edges. Everyone will be fully supported by the parachute and the weight of the other players. Use teacher discretion for this activity!

Rainbow Run

Have players choose their favourite colour, or assign each player a colour. Everyone slowly billows the parachute up and down. When the parachute is lifted, call out a colour and have those players run under the parachute to the other side before the parachute goes down. Encourage different travelling actions to pass under the parachute (e.g., crawling, walking, skipping, etc.).

Parachute Games

Toss It Off

Assign some players to grip the parachute edges and some players to stand around the outside. Throw a few balls or beanbags onto the parachute. Players holding the parachute must work together to toss the balls or beanbags off, and players around the outside work together to throw the balls or beanbags back on.

Popcorn Poppers

Have players practice lifting the parachute above their heads and back down in a fast, smooth motion. Then throw light balls on top of the parachute and launch them into the air

Ocean Tale

Tell a dramatic story about a ship on the ocean. Have players make large, medium, or small moves with the parachute to match the type of waves in the story.

Switcheroo

Direct all players to hold onto the edges of the parachute and billow it up and down. Call the names of two players who are at opposite sides of the parachute. The two players run under the parachute, high five each other as they meet underneath, then continue across to the opposite side to take each other's place.

Catch a Wave

Throw a beach ball on top of the parachute and have players move it around by making different sizes of waves.

Jaws

Choose a player to be the first Jaws. The rest of the players will grip the edges of the parachute and hold it at waist height. Jaws goes under the parachute and holds one hand pointed upward above his or her head to look like a shark fin pushing against the parachute. Jaws moves around, while the other players make the sounds of waves and make waves with the parachute. Jaws moves quickly to "bite" a player by grabbing their leg and that player goes under the parachute to become a second Jaws. Now both players can grab other players. The game ends when everyone has been brought under the parachute.

Yoga

Yoga is a wonderful form of exercise to calm the mind, and warm, stretch, and strengthen the muscles and body. Slow movements gently increase breathing and blood flow, which in turn fuels the muscles and tissues and increases flexibility. Children benefit from gentle stretching and movement that is done in a calm and quiet manner, leaving children feeling calm, peaceful, flexible, and ready to take on more vigorous and strenuous activities. Remember that every body is different, so each child's pose might also look a little different from their neighbour's pose. The emphasis should not be on performing perfect poses, and should be adapted as needed for individual children.

Getting Started

- Ideally, children should wear comfortable clothing and practice in bare feet on individual yoga mats or soft grass.
- You may want to set the tone for yoga by playing soft, soothing music.
- Ensure that children have enough personal space to participate.
- Be a good role model and always demonstrate the poses for children, rather than just explaining what to do.
- Do not expect children to remember how to do the various poses. Be patient and review. You may ask children to show and explain the poses they know.

About Breathing

- Breathing deeply and steadily is important in yoga because it gives us energy for our body, and keeps us calm and focused.
- Remember to breathe in through your nose, down into your belly. Feel your belly get bigger as you breathe in, and get smaller again as you breathe out.
- Try to always breathe out through your nose. If you are working really hard, you may need to breath out through your mouth.

More Ideas

- Encourage children to be creative and invent their own unique poses and movements. Invite children to teach their peers their creations.
- Tell imaginative stories as a springboard for doing different yoga poses. For example, pretend you are going on a trip through the forest. Do poses such as a Tree, Frog, etc., as they come up in the story.

Yoga Pose Practice

Tree Pose

Let's become tall and strong
like a tree.

1. Stand straight, with your arms at your sides and feet together.
2. Imagine your feet are the roots, deep in the soil.
3. Breathe in. Lift your arms out at your sides. This will help you balance. Pull your belly button in to your spine for a strong tree trunk.
4. Shift your weight to one leg.
5. Slide your other foot up that leg, and place the bottom of your foot against your thigh or below your knee. Turn your knee out.
6. Lift and stretch your arms upward like the branches of a tree growing in the sun.
7. Then, bring your hands down in front of your chest, and press your palms together in the salutation pose.

Yoga Pose Practice

Rainbow Pose

Let's show off all the beautiful colours of the rainbow.

1. Either kneeling or standing, breathe in while raising both arms over your head.
2. Lower one arm. Slowly breathe out as you sweep the other arm over your head toward the opposite shoulder to make a rainbow shape.
3. Hold this position. Pull in your belly button to keep your rainbow big, beautiful, and bright. Show off all the colours!
4. Breathe in as you slowly straighten your body and return to the starting position.
5. Now make a rainbow with your other arm.

Yoga Pose Practice

Mountain Pose

Let's stand tall like a mighty mountain.

1. Stand tall with feet together, or feet wider apart. Point your toes forward.
2. Have your arms down at your sides.
3. Press your shoulders back.
4. Make your body tall, straight, and strong, like a mighty mountain.
5. Breathe in and out deeply and slowly.

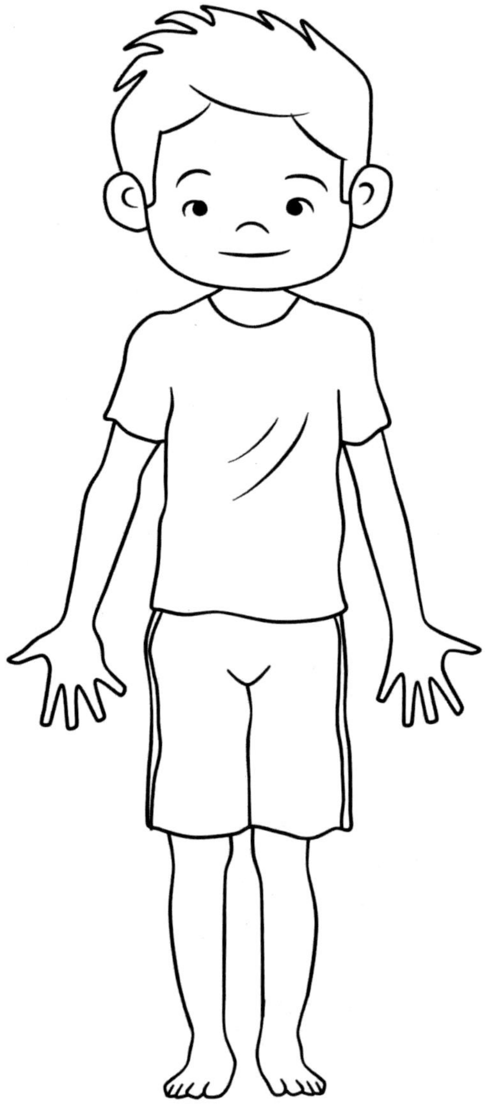

Yoga Pose Practice

Child Pose

Let's rest our bodies on the floor like a little child.

1. Kneel on the floor with your feet together, and flatten your feet out behind you, toenails on the floor.
2. Sit back on your heels with your knees slightly apart.
3. Slowly lower your forehead to the floor. Keep your bottom on your heels.
4. Place your arms beside your body toward the back, with your palms facing up.
5. Hold the pose. Then relax your body like a sleeping baby, quiet and peaceful. Then slowly sit up again.

Crocodile Pose

Let's lift our chest like a crocodile opening its mouth.

1. Lie on your tummy with your forehead touching the ground, your feet stretched out behind you, and squeezing your bottom.
2. Bring your arms in front of your head, then place each hand on your arm at the elbow. Rest your forehead on your arms.
3. Breathe in through your nose as you lift your chest from the ground nice and high like when a crocodile is opening its big mouth.
4. Breathe out as you bring your upper body back to the floor.

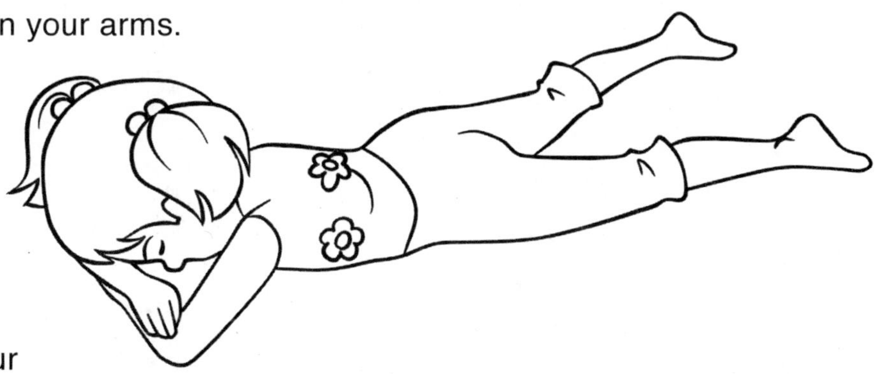

Yoga Pose Practice

Camel Pose

Let's lift up our chest high like the hump of a camel.

1. Go on your knees on the floor with your feet flat out behind you, toenails on the floor.
2. Keep your body straight.
3. Place the palm of your hands on your lower back. Squeeze your bottom as you push your hips forward. Try to keep your hips over your knees.
4. Gently look up and arch your back and reach back behind you.
5. Lift your chest like a camel's hump.

Shooting Stars

Let's make stars twinkle as they shoot through the sky.

1. Sit strong and tall, and pull your belly button to your spine. Cross your legs.
2. As you breathe in, reach your hands up above your head, palms facing each other.
3. As you breathe out, wiggle your fingers like little stars twinkling, while you slowly bring your hands back down with your arms out wide.
4. Repeat.

Yoga Pose Practice

Frog Pose

Let's squat like a frog ready to leap over a log.

1. Stand with your feet shoulder-width apart, and squat down.
2. While balancing on your toes, keep your knees spread wide apart.
3. Put your hands on the floor between your knees.
4. Look straight ahead and breathe in. You are just like a frog. Say "ribbit!"
5. As you breathe out, keep you hands on the floor while you straighten your legs so your bottom goes up. Lower your head toward your knees.
6. Come back to the squatting position, and repeat.

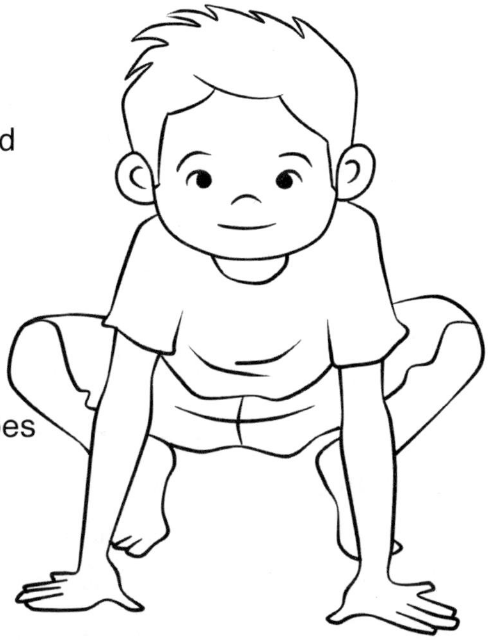

Lion Pose

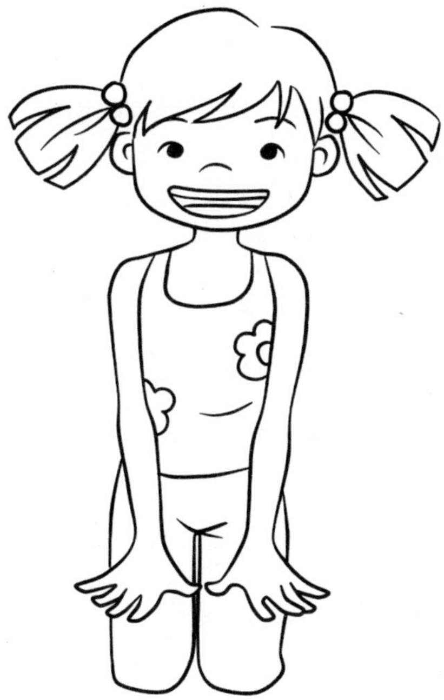

Let's become a lion, the mighty king of the jungle.

1. Kneel on the floor and sit back on your feet.
2. Place your hands on your thighs and stretch your arms.
3. Spread your fingers, flare your nostrils, and open your eyes wide.
4. Open your mouth wide like a big lion yawning and stick out your tongue.
5. Curl the tip of your tongue toward your chin. Breathe in deeply.
6. Exhale with a roar just like a mighty lion!

Yoga Pose Practice

Fish Pose

Let's puff out our chest like a fish breathing through its gills.

1. Lie on the floor on your back, with your knees bent and your feet flat on the floor.
2. Lift your bottom slightly off the floor. Slide your hands, palms down, under your bottom and move your arms under your body. Lower your body so your bottom sits on the backs of your hands.
3. Press your forearms and elbows firmly against the floor. Squeeze your shoulder blades together.
4. Take a breath in. Arch your back to lift your back and head away from the floor.
5. Gently let the crown or back of your head rest on the floor. Keep your head touching the floor only very lightly to avoid hurting your neck. Press your heels forward. Keep the weight on your elbows to keep the weight off your head.
6. Imagine you are breathing through fish gills.
7. Breathe out. Press into your elbows again and slide your head gently back, returning your body and head to the floor.

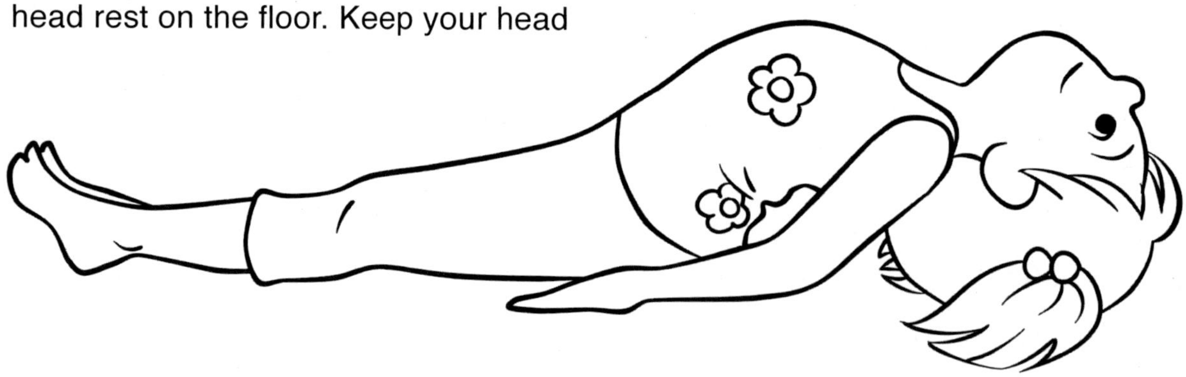

Yoga Pose Practice

Cat Pose

Let's stretch and warm up our spine by pretending to be our favourite kitty.

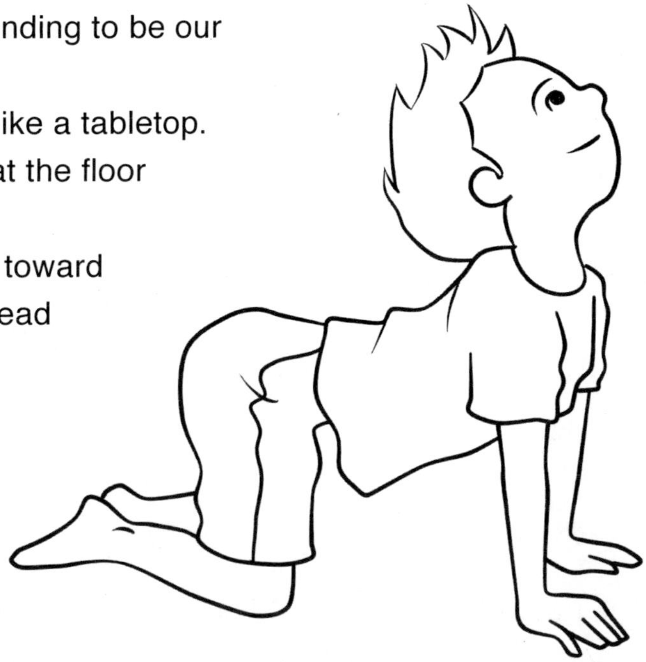

1. Go on your hands and knees on the floor like a tabletop.
2. Flatten your back and look straight down at the floor below you.
3. As you breathe in, drop your tummy down toward the floor like a cat and slowly lift up your head and neck so you are looking forward.
4. As you exhale, lift up your tummy and spine so your back is arched like a cat stretching. Bend your neck and look toward your belly button.
5. Finish by flattening your back and looking straight down at the floor below you.

Kite Pose

Let's become a kite flying high in the sky.

1. Stand up straight with your feet wide apart.
2. Breathe in as you lift your arms out to your sides. Slowly lift your left foot off the floor.
3. Breathe out as you lean to the side and lift your left leg higher. Steady your eyes to help keep your balance.
4. You are like a kite! Feel the warm sun. Your breath out is the wind.
5. Keep pulling your belly button to your spine for a strong tummy.
6. Lower your foot to the floor and stand with your feet and arms spread wide.
7. Repeat the pose with the right leg.

Nature Walk Focus Ideas

Nature Walks

Nature walks are a fun and effective way for children to immerse themselves into the outdoor environment. During a nature walk, children can search for different objects of nature using their different senses. Allow children to take digital photos of what they find and then display photos as a class collage, or sort according to different rules and categories. On other occasions, educators may wish for children to collect items into a bucket, or paper bag to later share their discoveries.

Suggested Read Aloud

"I Took a Walk" by Henry Cole

Finding Symmetry in Nature

The natural world is full of lines of symmetry, for example, leaves, snowflakes, fruit, vegetables, and insects. Present to children examples of symmetry such as flowers or leaves, pictures of animals or butterflies. Explain to children that symmetry means precisely the same on each side reflected as mirror images. While on a nature walk, have children collect or take photos of various objects from nature such as flowers leaves, sticks, tree stumps, pinecones, rocks, shells, etc. In a whole group, have children present their objects or photos and talk about why they think their findings are symmetrical. As an extension activity, stick down a piece of string on the ground to make a mirror line. Talk with children about producing their own symmetrical patterns using pairs of objects from the nature walk that have been sorted as a class, on either side of the line.

Suggested Read Aloud

"What Is Symmetry in Nature?" by Bobbie Kalman

Nature Walk Focus Ideas

Patterns in Nature

Nature is full of patterns that can be observed and described. Brainstorm with children a list of simple predictable patterns in nature such as how each day the sky changes from morning to night. The sun comes up, and then the sun goes down. The leaves on trees change in a pattern as the seasons change. Other patterns that can be observed and described include veins in a leaf, spirals on a shell, flower petals, tree bark and much more. Keep a class learning log of these findings. In addition, some objects of nature may be ideal to use for printmaking.

Suggested Read Aloud

"The Seasons of Arnold's Apple Tree" by Gail Gibbons

Sounds in Nature

Sounds are around us. In this activity, children practice mindful listening. Mindful listening helps children to choose which specific sounds to focus their attention on. As children learn to self- monitor how to focus their attention, they build self-management skills and are more able to listen in a focused way to what people are saying. Ask children if they know which animals have the best sense of hearing such as owls.

As children guess, give various clues to "the owl" such as "bird," says "hoo," etc. Explain to children that an owl's sense of hearing is more sensitive than a human's hearing they go out at night to hunt. They can hear from far away, and owls have uneven ears that help determine sound coming from different directions. Have children go on a nature walk with a focus on listening for sounds that are close by and far away. Then come together as a group and share the sounds they heard. Some discussion prompts include: What kind of sounds did they hear far away? What kind of sounds did they hear close by? What sounds cam from living things? What sounds came from non-living things? What types of sounds do they hear if they sit silently for thirty seconds versus walking around and listening?

Suggested Read Aloud Materials

"The Listening Walk" by Paul Showers

Signs of Spring Survey

The temperature is getting warmer.	Yes	No
The trees are growing leaves.	Yes	No
The grass is green.	Yes	No
The sun sets later.	Yes	No
The birds are returning.	Yes	No
Farmers are planting crops.	Yes	No
Animals that hibernate in the winter come out.	Yes	No
We have some rainy weather and puddles.	Yes	No
Plants begin to sprout.	Yes	No
The snow has melted.	Yes	No
We sometimes wear raincoats and jackets.	Yes	No

Is it spring? Explain your thinking.

____

____

________________________ 's Spring Scavenger Hunt!

Circle all the things you can see, hear, smell or touch.

<table>
<tr><td>
Seeds or Nuts</td><td>
Birds Singing</td><td>
Flowers</td><td>
Plant Buds</td></tr>
<tr><td>
Grass</td><td>
Earthworm</td><td>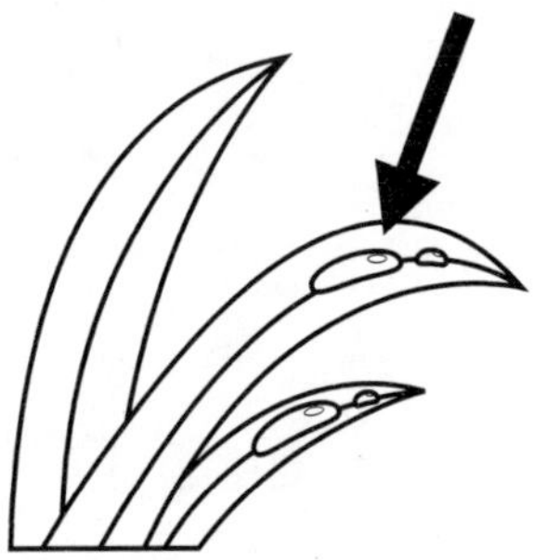
Dew</td><td>
Green Leaves</td></tr>
<tr><td>
Puddle</td><td>
An animal</td><td>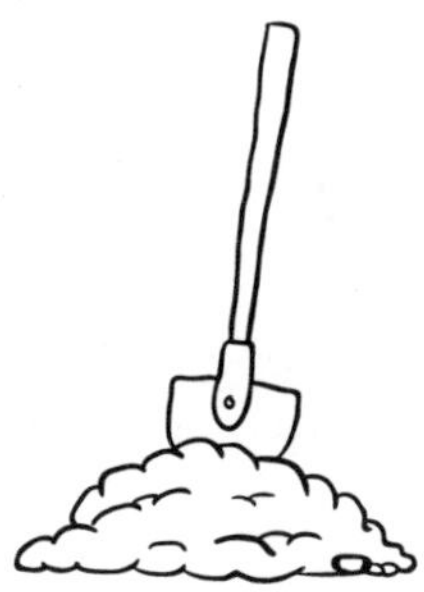
Fresh Soil</td><td>
Feather</td></tr>
</table>

Signs of Summer Survey

The temperature is usually hot.	Yes	No
Plants are growing.	Yes	No
The grass is green.	Yes	No
The days are long.	Yes	No
There are lots of animals outside.	Yes	No
Flowers are blooming.	Yes	No
The air feels humid.	Yes	No
There is less rain.	Yes	No
We spend lots of time outside.	Yes	No
There are lots of insects.	Yes	No
We wear shorts, hats and t-shirts.	Yes	No

Is it summer? Explain your thinking.

____

____

________________'s Summer Scavenger Hunt!

Circle all the things you can see, hear, smell or touch.

 Dandelions	 Warm Sun on Your Face	 Butterfly	 Birds Singing
 A Leaf Bigger Than Your Hand	 Green Grass	 Flowers	 Fluffy White Cloud
 Bird Nest	 Dragonfly	 Minibeast	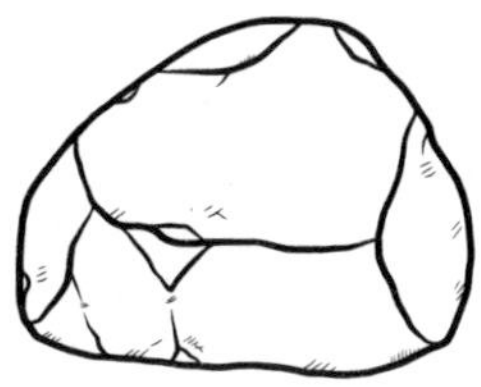 Rock

Signs of Autumn Survey

The air is becoming cooler.	Yes	No
The sun is setting earlier.	Yes	No
The days are getting shorter.	Yes	No
The leaves are changing colour.	Yes	No
The leaves are beginning to fall.	Yes	No
The birds are ready to fly south.	Yes	No
The crops are ready for harvest.	Yes	No
Soon we will celebrate Thanksgiving.	Yes	No
The squirrels are storing food.	Yes	No
The grass is wet with dew.	Yes	No
We wear jackets to stay warm.	Yes	No

Is it autumn? Explain your thinking.

_______________________'s Autumn Scavenger Hunt!

Circle all the things you can see, hear, smell or touch.

 Brown Leaf	 Yellow Leaf	 Red Leaf	 Dry Leaf
 Pinecone	 Acorn	 Tree Bark	 Tree Roots
 Feather	 Grass	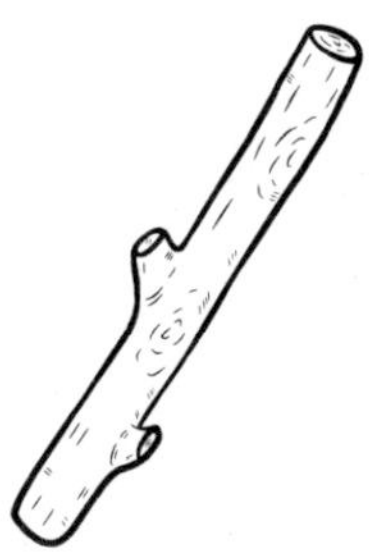 Stick	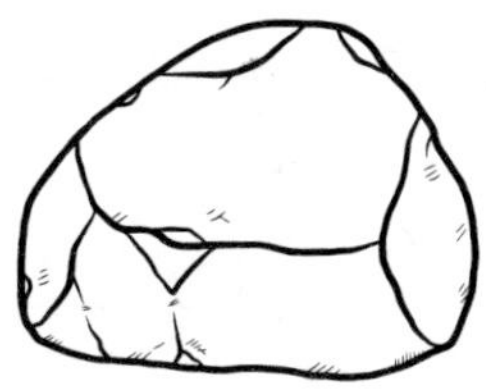 Rock

Signs of Winter Survey

The temperature is cold.	Yes	No
The trees are bare.	Yes	No
The ground feels hard and cold.	Yes	No
There are less birds.	Yes	No
The ground can be icy and slippery.	Yes	No
Soon we will celebrate the New Year.	Yes	No
There is snowy and windy weather.	Yes	No
Plants stop growing.	Yes	No
There is less sunlight.	Yes	No
The grass is covered with snow.	Yes	No
We wear coats, mittens and hats.	Yes	No

Is it winter? Explain your thinking.

____________________'s Winter Scavenger Hunt!

Circle all the things you can see, hear, smell or touch.

 Icicle	 Snow	 Bird	 Pinecone
 Pine Needles	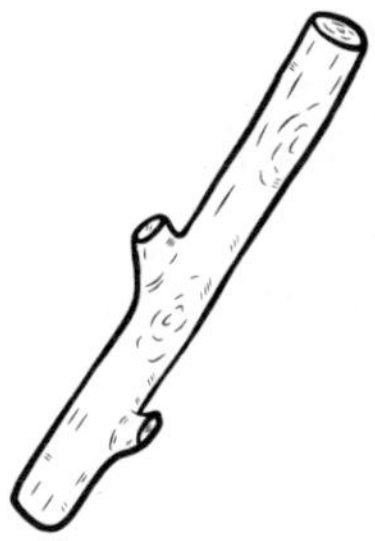 Twig	 Footprints	 Animal Tracks
 Tree Bark	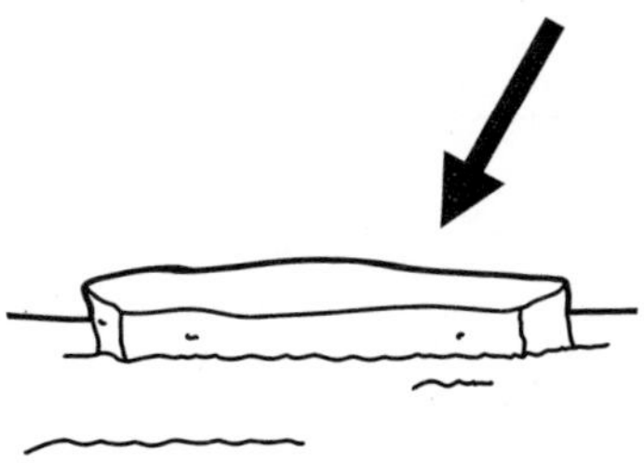 Ice	 A Tree Without Leaves	 An Evergreen Tree

______________'s Living and Non-living Things Hunt

Explore Outside

Draw and label the things you find that are living and non-living things.

Make a Prediction

Will you find more living or non-living things on your hunt?

- ❑ Living things
- ❑ Non-living things

Living

Non-Living

Was your prediction correct? ❑ Yes ❑ No

Write about your observations.

____

____

________________________'s Texture Nature Hunt

We touch and feel with out hands and skin.

Explore Outside

Draw and label the things you find that have these textures.

Something Smooth	Something Rough
Something Hard	Something Soft
Something Wet	Something Dry
Something Sticky	Something Bumpy

______________________________ 's Nature Shape Hunt

No matter where you live, you can see different shapes outside in nature.

Explore Outside

Draw and label the things you spot that have these shapes.

● Circle	■ Square

▲ Triangle	▬ Rectangle

______________________________'s Nature Shape Hunt

No matter where you live, you can see different shapes outside in nature.

Explore Outside

Draw and label the things you find that have these shapes.

⬮ **Oval**	◆ **Diamond**
⬢ **Hexagon**	**Other?**

Common Animal Tracks Hunt

Can you find any of the tracks below?

 Domestic House Cat	 Domestic Dog	 Mouse	 Rabbit
 Goose	 Fox	 Squirrel	 Deer
 Sparrow	 Seagull	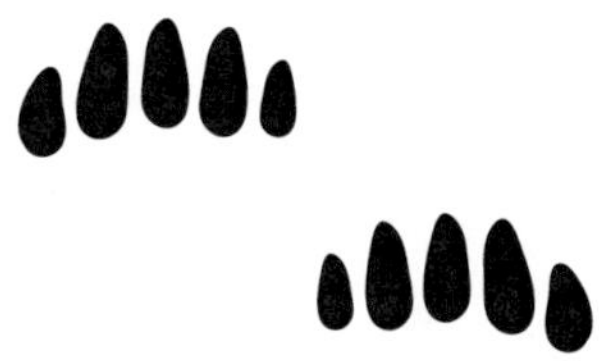 Mole	 Raccoon

Canadian Leaf Hunt

Can you find any of the leaves below?

 **Maple**	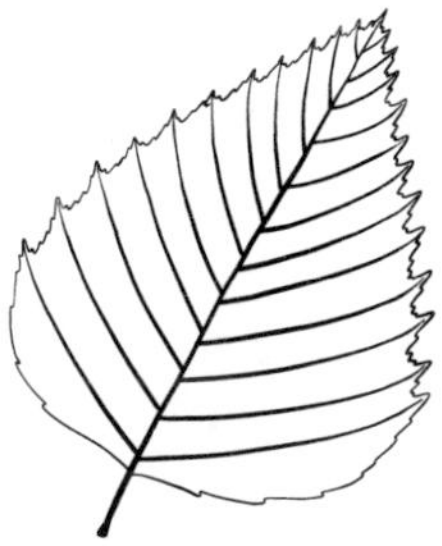 **Birch**	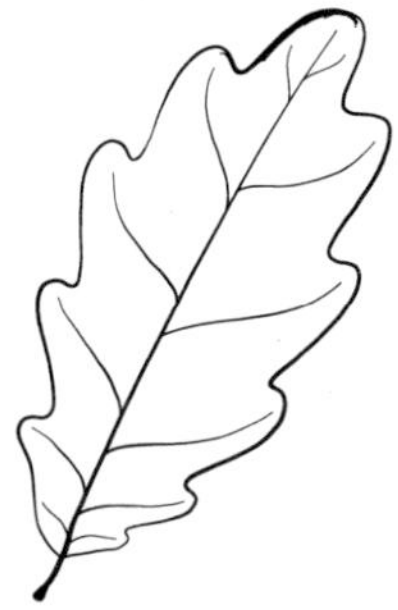 **Oak**	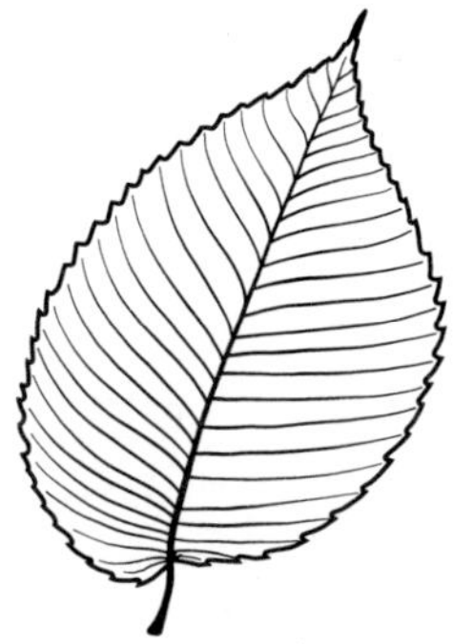 **Elm**
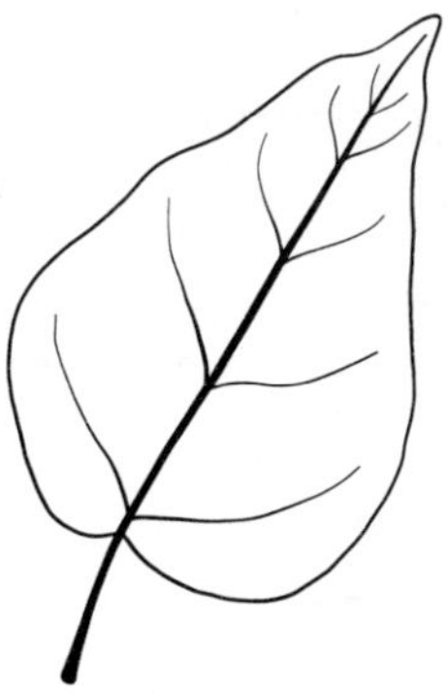 **Lilac**	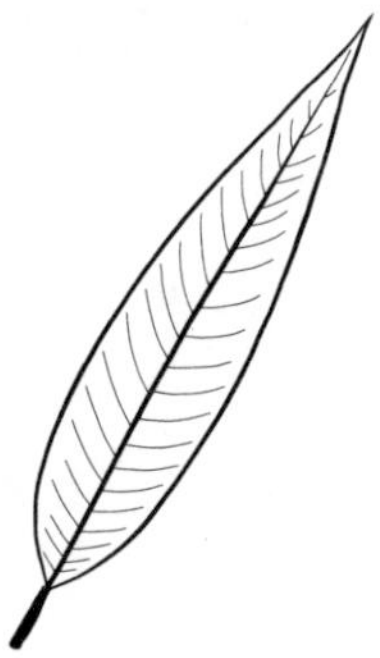 **Willow**	 **Ash**	 **Aspen**
 **Linden**	 **Poplar**	 **Rowan**	 **Magnolia**

 |

Outdoor Scavenger Hunt Cards

Find 7 green leaves.

Find 2 acorns.

Arrange 10 rocks into a circle.

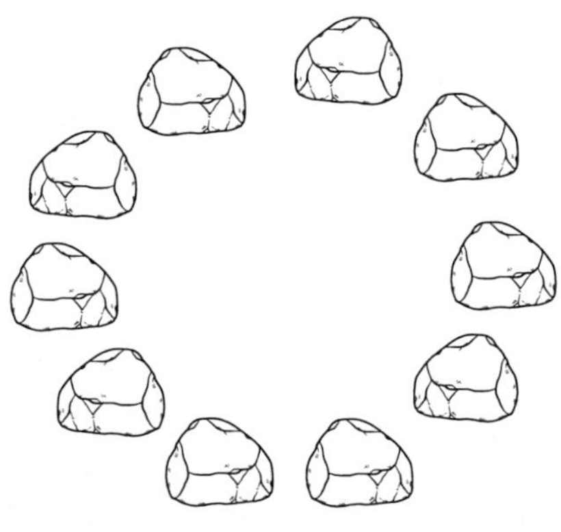

Find 1 feather.

Outdoor Scavenger Hunt Cards

Find 9 nuts or seeds.

Arrange 3 sticks into a triangle.

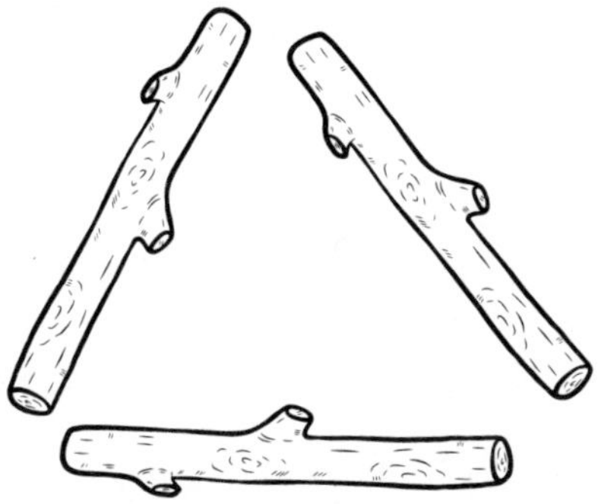

Find 5 flowers growing.

Arrange 4 pine needles into a square.

Outdoor Scavenger Hunt Cards

Find 6 diffrent types of leaves.

Find 3 pinecones.

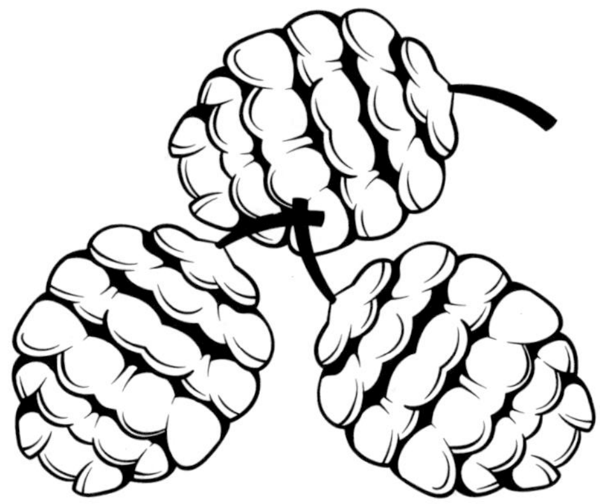

Arrange 6 sticks into a rectangle.

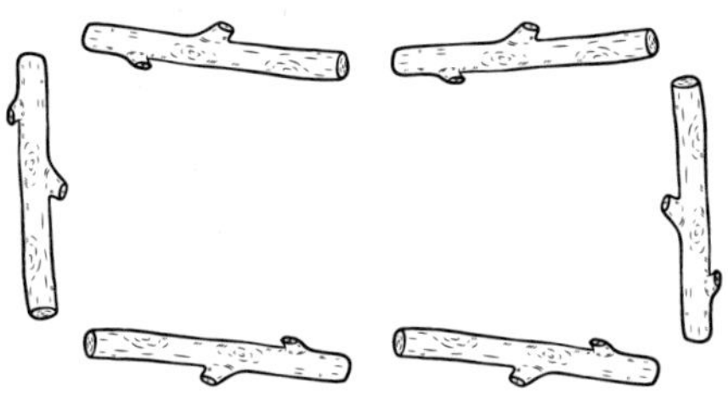

Find 1 maple leaf.

Outdoor Activities for Spring

Colour Match

Collect paint chips from a local hardware or paint store. Provide children with a range of different colours and have them hunt for objects of nature or materials in the outdoor classroom that match the different paint chips.

Spring Flower Pots

Have students bring in flower pots. Provide soil and flower seeds for children to use for planting. Review the process of growing a flower plant. Keep a learning log of observations as the seed grows to a flower.

Natural Paint Brush

Encourage children to collect a variety of thick leaves. Tie leaves together to create a bunch. Attach the bunch to the end of a stick and paint away!

Build a Bird Feeder

Provide children with a variety of recycled materials, tape and string. Instruct children to design and create a bird feeder. Fill feeders with seeds and hang them from trees in the outdoor classroom.

Bird Watch Tally

Brainstorm or provide children with a chart of different kinds of birds found in your area. Ask children to tally the various birds they spot in the outdoor classroom. Discuss similar and different characteristics of the birds observed. Keep a class learning log.

Seed Match

Bring in a variety of seeds for children to examine. Print out pictures of the plants each type of seed aligns with. Instruct children to guess which seeds grow into which plant or flower.

Outdoor Activities for Spring

Class Garden

Plant a class garden. Find a defined area in the outdoor classroom. Introduce the concept of class garden. Outline the steps of planting a garden:

1. weeding the garden and prepping the soil
2. planting seeds and/or plants, mulching
3. watering, weeding
4. harvesting

Decide as a class what you will plant. Enlist helpers from the school community to support the garden through donations of gardening tools, seeds, soil etc. Organize a schedule for taking care of the garden. Keep a class learning log of progress.

Suggested Read Aloud

"Up in the Garden and Down in the Dirt" by Kate Messner

Spring Things Collage

Ask children to collect a variety of items that represent spring. Provide children with a sheet protector or clear contact tape. Using glue or tape ask children to arrange their items in a creative way. Hang collages in the windows of the classroom or using clothes pins and string them up along a fence outside.

Spring Sensory Bottles

Instruct children to collect one natural item that represents spring. Use recycled bottles, allow children to place their item in a bottle and then fill it with water. Hot glue the lid onto the bottle to avoid leaks. Add a pinch of glitter or sparkles for an enhanced visual effect. Let children shake, play and examine their sensory bottles.

Nature Weaving

Create a natural wooden frame using four sticks tied together. Using thin strong string tie. Bring the string over the top of the frame, wrapping it around vertically and tying it on the bottom. Do this along the whole frame and try to space the string evenly across. Invite children to weave natural items into the frame.

Rock Decorating

Invite children to find a rock to decorate. Provide children with a variety of materials paint, markers, googly eyes and other craft supplies. Encourage children to turn their rocks into pet rock creatures.

Outdoor Activities for Summer

Flower Hunt

Have children walk around the outdoor classroom and identify all the different types of flowers in the yard. On a class chart, have children tally the different types of flowers. Discuss the similarities and differences between flowers using observational skills.

Soil Samples

Ask children to collect soil from different parts of the outdoor classroom. Place soil sample on white paper or newsprint. Compare the colour, texture and density of the soil. Predict which soil is the best for growing.

Bug Hunt

Brainstorm or provide children with a chart of different types of bugs. Ask children to tally the various bugs they spot in the outdoor classroom. Allow children to catch bugs to be examined using mesh nets. Discuss similar and different characteristics of the bugs observed. Release bugs back into their natural environment.

Sun Melting

Fill a muffin tin or tray with various items, some which will melt in the sun (i.e. crayons, toys, ice cube, marker, piece of chocolate, butter, coin, marble etc.). Ask children to predict which items will melt. Place the items in direct sunlight and record observations.

Outdoor Activities for Summer

Build an Insect Hotel

Explore the types of habitats that already exist in your outdoor classroom. Challenge children to design and build an insect hotel using natural materials from the outdoor classroom such as twigs, pinecone, grass, pebbles etc. Provide children with recycled containers, string, straw or hay. Discuss with children what else they might add to their insect hotel to attract creatures such as sugar cubes etc. Share homes through a gallery walk and observe what creatures have come to visit.

Summer Soup

Ask children to collect various natural items that represent summer (i.e. flower petals, twigs, leaves, grass, seeds.) In a big pot let children mix their items together to create a summer soup. Let children observe and play with their creation, but make sure they don't taste it!

Shadow Art

On a sunny day, pair children into duos and provide them with a piece of chalk. Have one partner stand in a pose and challenge the other partner to trace his or her shadow. Switch roles and admire creations through a gallery walk.

Mystery Bulb

Show children how to plant a bulb and encourage them to predict what it will become. Plant the bulb somewhere in the outdoor classroom. Encourage children to water and care for the bulb. Allow children to continue to guess until the plant blooms.

Sediment Jar

Invite children to collect a sample of soil. Mix the soil in a jar and then leave it to settle for a few days. Notice the varying layers of the soil and draw and label each one.

Outdoor Activities for Autumn

Leaf Printmaking

Have children pick a leaf from the outdoor classroom. Instruct children to press their leaf onto a paper plate with paint carefully. Next, press the painted leaf onto a piece of paper. Encourage children to create interesting arrangements of the leaves. Also, as a whole group, compare how their leaf print is similar or different from their real leaf.

Bark Rubbings

Using crayons with wrappers removed, instruct children to create rubbings with different tree bark. The rough texture of the bark of a tree is an excellent way to introduce children to surfaces and textures in their natural environment.

Tree Cookies

Present children with tree cookies of various sizes and shapes. Discuss how a tree grows a new layer of bark each year. The rings in a tree's bark mark how many layers of bark it has. Ask the children to determine the age of the tree based on the number of rings on each tree cookie.

Build A Tower

Challenge children to see who can build the tallest tower out of natural materials found in the outdoor classroom.

Leaf Sorting

Instruct children to collect leaves from the outdoor classroom and then sort them into different categories (i.e., colour, type, shape, texture). Next, create a graph using the leaves and the different categories.

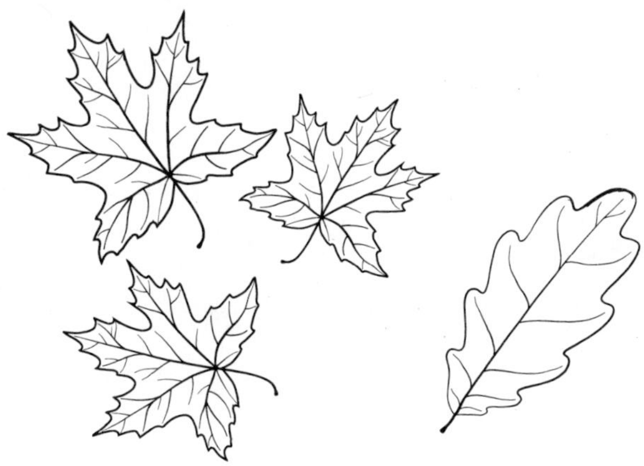

Outdoor Activities for Autumn

Fall Colour Tally

Using a T-chart, invite students to spot and tally all the different leaf colours in the outdoor classroom. Discuss which colour has the most leaves, which colour has the least amount of leaves and why this could be.

Tree Tally Tracker

Have children walk around the outdoor classroom and identify all the different types of trees in the yard. On a class chart, have children tally the different kinds of trees. Discuss the similarities and differences between trees using observation skills. Prompt children to consider tree sizes, colours, textures, heights, leaves, etc. Discuss the differences of coniferous versus deciduous trees.

Leaf Pile Up

Discuss with children what they think happens to leaves in the winter. Explain to children why people often pick up leaves that fall to protect the grass in their yards. Provide children with rakes and gloves and ask them to pile leaves in the outdoor classroom. Challenge groups of students to collect the most leaves and make the tallest pile.

Twig Raft

Instruct children to gather twigs around the outdoor classroom. Provide children with yarn and scissors. Challenge children to build a raft out of twigs that will float in a bin of water. Test out rafts and record observations on a class chart.

Outdoor Activities for Winter

Snow Design

Offer children a variety of recycled spray and squirt bottles. Fill each bottle with water and a different colour of food colouring. Have children create designs, messages, and drawings in the snow.

Catching Snowflakes

Provide each child with a piece of black construction paper. Invite children to "catch snowflakes" onto their construction paper for inspection. Encourage children to use a magnifying lens to observe snowflakes up close. After children carefully examine their snowflakes, have them sketch some the structures they see and compare with others.

Ice Block Treasure

Place a few small toys or items into a container of water and freeze it overnight. Provide children with a variety of tools, plastic hammers, dull chisels, wooden blocks, etc. Allow children to chip away chunks of ice and free the items from the ice block.

Measuring Snow

Provide children with a ruler or meter stick. Encourage them to walk around the outdoor classroom measuring the height of snow from the ground up. Challenge children to build the tallest snow pile and measure it together.

Snow and Water

Ask children to gather a snow sample in a bucket and measure its density. Place the bucket in direct sunlight or bring it inside. Observe and record the snow turning into water. Measure how much water results from the melting of the snow.

Outdoor Activities for Winter

Melting Ice

Ask children to brainstorm different ways to melt ice. Test out melting ice with the sun, sand, and salt. Discuss which substance works the fastest.

Snow Volcano

In small groups have children build a volcano structure out of snow around an empty container. Once the volcano structure is built, fill the container with vinegar, food colouring followed by baking soda. Watch the volcano explode out and onto the snow.

Snow Maze

Provide children with shovels have them create a maze out of snow. Encourage them to create dead ends and multiple pathways but only one entrance and exit.

Build an Inukshuk

Show children a picture of an Inuksuk and explain that this is a structure made of stone shaped like a person that Inuit would use as landmarks in the Arctic. Instruct children to collect rocks and build their Inukshuk.

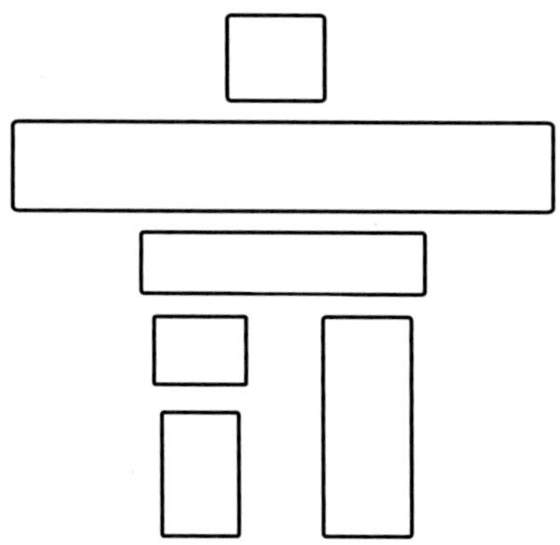

Peanut Free Bird Feeder

Have children take a toilet paper roll and cover it with a thick layer of lard. Explain to children that birds need fat to stay warm in the winter and the lard will provide that. Next, put bird seed on a plate. Roll the paper roll in the bird seed, making sure it sticks to the lard. Then, string a piece of yarn through paper roll. Finally, hang the paper rolls onto the trees and watch for birds to come and feed.

Marvelous Magnification

In this activity, children will learn how a magnifying lens can help them observe things that are too small to see with their eyes alone.

Materials

- magnifying lens for each child
- recording sheets and pencils
- 1m length of yarn or string for each child

Getting Started

If children have not explored with a magnifying lens before, build in some time for children to just play and explore with it. Help children to discover how a magnifying lens helps people see things in their surroundings by making things bigger. For example, have children examine the patterns on their fingertips. Encourage children to compare looking at other objects with a magnifying lens very carefully and then further away. Is there a difference in what they see? How?

Explore Outside

1. Encourage children to imagine and then discuss what they think it would be like to hike across the outdoor classroom as a small creature (i.e., ant, worm, beetle). How would the point of view of the tiny creature be different from theirs?

2. Next, explain to children that they are going to "shrink" down to the size of a tiny creature and "zoom" in on the natural environment to take a hike.

3. Then, give each child a metre long piece of string to mark their miniature hiking trail somewhere in the outdoor classroom. Ask them to find and observe things that would be hard to see without their magnifying lens and draw them onto their recording sheet. Encourage children to look for signs of life. For example exploring the cracks and crevices of the sidewalk, or looking under leaves.

_______________ 's Marvelous Magnification

Here is a picture of what I saw through the magnifying lens.

My observations...

Hula Hoop Observation

In this activity, children will have the opportunity to practice their **observation skills.**

Materials

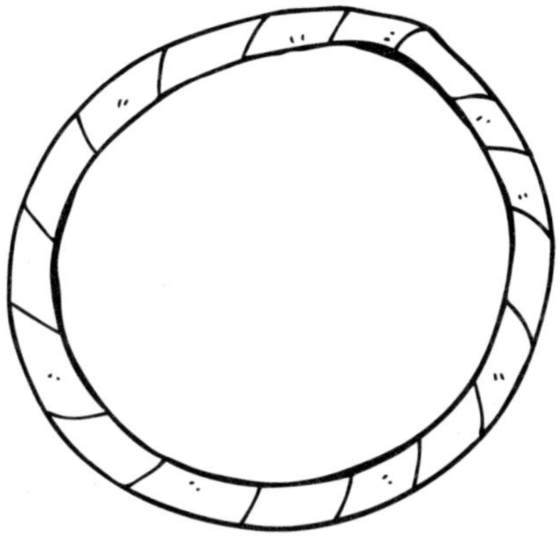

- hula hoops
- magnifying lens
- clipboards with sheets for drawing
- pencils
- word cards

Getting Started

Ideally, for this activity divide children into groups of three or four. Instruct children that they will be using a hula hoop to mark a spot for observation in the outdoor classroom. Explain that their job will be to make a detailed drawing of the natural environment that they observe within their hula hoop.

Explore Outside

1. Give each child or a small group of children a hula hoop.
2. Allow children to place it anywhere in the outdoor classroom.
3. Encourage children to look closely into their hula hoop are and draw or note all the natural materials they see.
4. Instruct children to label their drawings using appropriate vocabulary (i.e., soil, insect, bark, dew, etc.)

Sharing Discoveries

Invite children to share their observations with the class. Use the questions below to facilitate the discussion.

- Identify items discovered as living/nonliving.
- Discuss signs of seasonal changes.
- Examine animal markings and explore habitats.
- How are the observations the same or different from group to group?

My Leaf Observation by ____________________

This is a ______________________________________ leaf.

This is a picture of my leaf.

My leaf is...

- red
- orange
- yellow
- green
- brown
- purple

I think the size of my leaf is...

☐ small

☐ medium

☐ large

This is what I notice about my leaf...

Are Leaves Alive?

Observe leaves from a distance and up close! Pick a leaf and tape it in the box.

I think that leaves: ❑ are living ❑ are not living

Because I observed ______________________________

and I know ______________________________

Think about it!

Are leaves on the ground the same as leaves on a tree?
Explain your thinking.

____

____

Leaf Necklace

Materials

- leaves
- small sticks
- scissors
- hole punch

Getting Started

1. Cut a length of string long enough for a loose necklace.
2. Tie a small stick to the end of the string - this will act as the needle. Tie a large knot at the other end of the string.
3. Instruct the children to pick their own leaves for their necklace. Direct them to make a pattern using a variety of different leaves including colour and size.
4. Create threading holes in the leaves with the hole punch or encourage the children to make the holes by themselves.
5. Once the leaves have been threaded into a necklace untie the stick and tie off the necklace.
6. Encourage the children to wear their necklaces.

Sharing Discoveries

Invite children to share their observations with the class. Use the questions below to facilitate the discussion:

- What materials were the most popular amongst the children?
- Why did children choose the materials they did?
- What do they like about their necklace
- What kind of patterns did they use to make their necklace?
- What leaves worked best? Why?

______________________ 's Minibeast Tracker

Explore Outside

Add a tally every time you see a minibeast.

Predicition

Where do you think you will spot the most minibeasts? ______________________

Name of Minibeast	On the Ground	On Plants	On Trees	Under Rocks	In the Air

Wildlife Watchers

Announce to children that as **wildlife watchers**, they will observe living creatures in the outdoor classroom. Explain that wildlife watching is the observation of animals in their natural habitats. It is crucial that children learn to observe without disrupting the creature's habitat or negatively interacting with the animal (i.e., chasing squirrels, picking up worms, catching butterflies). Reinforce with children that they should focus on observing from a distance while taking note of how the creature behaviours and interacts with the natural environment. Wildlife watching can be done with the naked eye, or with tools like binoculars or magnify lens.

Do's

- Observe from a distance.
- Be quiet, still and patient.
- Listen carefully.
- Blend into your surroundings.
- Record what you see.

Don'ts

- Do not touch the wildlife or it's home.
- Do not move anything out of its natural place.

Materials

- ❑ Clipboards with recording sheet
- ❑ Pencils
- ❑ Magnifying Lens (optional)
- ❑ Binoculars (optional)

Explore Outside

Encourage children to find a quiet, almost hidden spot to look for living creatures. Prompt children to patiently observe all around them until they catch a glimpse of an animal or insect. Instruct children to record their observations using the wildlife watching log.

Share Discoveries

Invite children to share their observations with the class. Use the questions below to facilitate the discussion.

- What living creature did you observe?
- Where do you think it lives?
- What do you think it eats?
- Does the weather influence whether we will see this creature?
- What do you think the wildlife was attempting to do?

_______________________ 's Wildlife Watching Log

The season is: ❑ Spring ❑ Summer ❑ Autumn ❑ Winter

The weather is:

Location ____

I am observing ____

This is a picture of what I observe.

Notes

____

____

____

 |

Build a Nest

Materials Needed

- mud/ dirt
- water
- sticks/ twigs
- grass
- leaves

Getting Started

Ideally, for this activity divide children into groups of one or two. Challenge children to create a nest using only natural materials (mud, grass, sticks, leaves). Encourage them to make the nest large enough for a robin or blue jay. Encourage them to make the nest warm and safe enough for eggs.

Explore Outside

1. Direct children to explore the nearby area and look for natural materials.
2. Allow the children to decide how they want to make their nest, encourage their ideas and assist them if they are not sure where to start.

Sharing Discoveries

Invite children to share their observations with the class. Use the questions below to facilitate the discussion.:

- What materials were the easiest to build with?
- Why did children choose the materials they did?
- What do they like about their nest?
- What could they do to improve their nest?
- What kind of bird do they think will use it?

____________________'s Bird Watching Tracker

Explore Outside

Add a tally every time you see one of these types of birds.

Prediction: Which bird do you think you will spot the most? ____________________

Bird	Tally
 **Robin**	
 **Sparrow**	
 **Chickadee**	
 **Bluejay**	
 **Cardinal**	

Super Soil Sleuth

In this activity, children have the opportunity to discover that not all soil have the same characteristics.

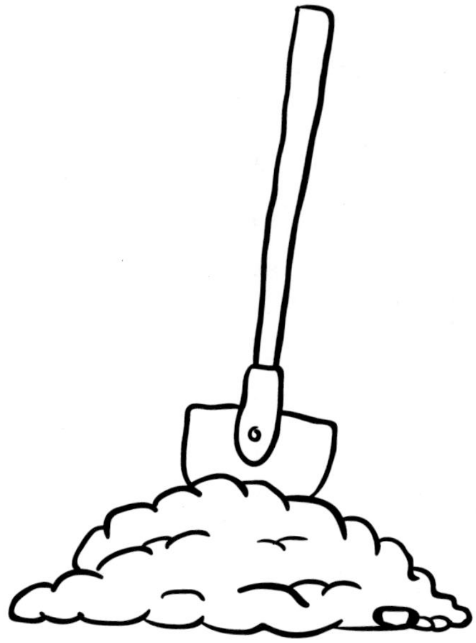

Materials

- two plastic bags
- a scoop to collect soil
- marker
- magnifying lens

Getting Started

1. Collect some soil from a location and place in a plastic bag: This is Soil Sample A
2. Using a marker write the name of the location of sample A on the plastic bag.
3. Next, collect some soil from a different location and place in a plastic bag. This is Soil Sample B.
4. Using a marker write the name of the location of sample B on the plastic bag.
5. Using the Super Soil Sleuth Examination sheet examine each sample of soil and record your findings.

Sharing Discoveries

Invite children to share their observations with the class. Use the questions below to facilitate the discussion.
- How are the soil samples the same/different?
- Which soil do you think would be best for growing plants? Explain.

Suggested Read Aloud

"Dirt: The Scoop on Soil" by Natalie M. Rosinsky

______________________'s Super Soil Tracker

Soil Sample	Sample A Location	Sample B Location
Colour		
Texture		
Weight		
Smell		
Other Observations		

How Do Animals Stay Warm in Winter?

Ask children how they think animals stay warm in the winter. Complete a class KWL chart and record each child's comment followed by his or her initials.

Discuss the ways humans stay warm in the winter (heated homes, winter coats, winter mittens, etc.). Prompt children to consider "If animals don't wear coats as we do, what do you think they do to stay warm?"

Explore Outside

- Prompt children to look for places that animals may find shelter to stay warm in the outdoor classroom.
- Create a blubber glove using lard and two plastic bags. Place one bag inside of the other. Spread the lard between the two bags and then tape the outer edges of the top. Tell children to take off their mitts and feel the cold air, then have them put on the blubber glove and note the difference. Explain that blubber is a layer of fat that can help animals stay warm.
- Ask children to consider how animal fur may be like our winter coats and mittens.

Sharing Discoveries

Invite children to share their observations and findings with the class. Record child answers on chart paper. Share different shelters children observed and explain how burrows can protect animals from the cold temperatures, snow, and ice. Also, discuss how animal fur is warm and acts as a winter coat. Explain that many animals grow thicker layers of fur during the winter months. Prompt children to think about animals and birds they may have seen gathering and eating lots of food in the winter. Discuss how this leads them to store extra layers of fat and draw connections to the blubber glove.

Suggested Read Alouds

"Animals in Winter" by Henrietta Bancroft and Richard G. Van Gelder
"When It Starts to Snow" by Phillis Gershator

How Do Animals Stay Warm in Winter?

Explore Outside

Do you see any animals? What part of their bodies would help them stay warm?

Draw and label your ideas.

I predict that animals stay warm by ____________________

because I observed ____________________

and I know ____________________

Think about it!

When you tried on the blubber glove how did it feel?

____

____

Does the Sun Move?

Explore Outside

Walk around outside and place a large stick vertically in the sunniest spot you can find. Find the stick's shadow and mark it with a rock. Observe the shadow and mark any movement you notice with a rock.

Darw what you see.

The sun ______________________________

because I observed ______________________________

and I know ______________________________

Think about it!

Does the sun move everyday? How do you know?

____

____

_______________________________ 's Inquiry Question

____

This is a picture of what I see.

I think ____

because I observed ____

and I know ____

____

______________________________'s

Seasonal Log

The season is:

Spring

Summer

Autumn

Winter

I wonder:

____

____

_______________________'s Senses Nature Walk

The season is:

Spring

Summer

Autumn

Winter

I see...

I hear...

I smell...

I feel...

______________________________'s Wildlife Sightings

The season is:

Spring Summer Autumn Winter

What?	When?

Where?

Notes

My Tree Observation

deciduous coniferous

The season is:

Spring Summer Autumn Winter

Here is an observational drawing of my tree.

Here is a detail I noticed about my tree.

______________________ 's Temperature Tracker

The season is:

Spring

Summer

Autumn

Winter

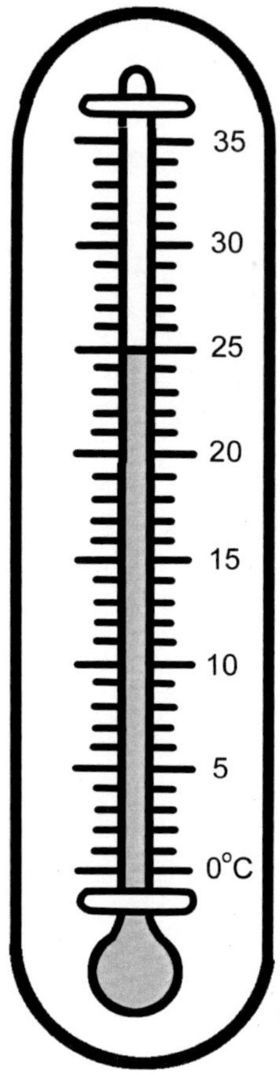

Getting Started

Does the temperature change through out the day?

Materials

Thermometer

Getting Started

1. Measure the outdoor temperature in the morning, at noon, and at the end of the day. Do this for five days.

2. Use the words below to fill in the blanks. A word can be used more than once.

cooler warmer

I predict that the temperature will be...

______________________________ in the morning.

______________________________ at noon.

______________________________ in the afternoon.

______________________ 's Temperature Tracker

1. With the help of an adult, record the results.

Day	Morning	Noon	Afternoon
1			
2			
3			
4			
5			

2. Does the temperature change during the day? Yes No

3. Fill in the blanks. Use the words below.

afternoon morning noon

The temperature is warmest at ______________________

The temperature is cooler in the ______________________

and the ______________________

______________________ 's Favourite thing

The season is:

Spring   Summer   Autumn   Winter

Write about it.

______________________________ 's Learning Log

The season is:

Spring Summer Autumn Winter

Draw a picture of something you learned.

Write about it.

____

____

____

____

___________________________'s Observation Tracker

The season is:

Spring   Summer   Autumn   Winter

I observed a ___________________________

Here is an observational drawing.

Colour ___________________________

Shape ___________________________

Size ___________________________

Texture ___________________________

Topic: ____________________

K What I Think I Already **Know**	W What I **Want** to Know	L What I **Learned**

 |

______________________________ 's Vocabulary

Keep a list of new words you have learned.

Make sure to include the definition for each word.

Word	Definition

How Am I Doing?

	Completing my work	Using my time wisely	Following directions	Keeping organized
Full Speed Ahead!	• My work is always complete and done with care. • I added extra details to my work.	• I always get my work done on time.	• I always follow directions.	• My materials are always neatly organized. • I am always prepared and ready to learn.
Keep Going!	• My work is complete and done with care. • I added extra details to my work.	• I usually get my work done on time.	• I usually follow directions without reminders.	• I usually can find my materials. • I am usually prepared and ready to learn.
Slow Down!	• My work is complete. • I need to check my work.	• I sometimes get my work done on time.	• I sometimes need reminders to follow directions.	• I sometimes need time to find my materials. • I am sometimes prepared and ready to learn.
Stop!	• My work is not complete. • I need to check my work.	• I rarely get my work done on time.	• I need reminders to follow directions.	• I need to organize my materials. • I am rarely prepared and ready to learn.

I am proud of ______________________________

I will work on ______________________________

Participation Rubric

Level	Child Participation Descriptor
4	Child consistently contributes to class discussions and activities by offering ideas and asking questions.
3	Child usually contributes to class discussions and activities by offering ideas and asking questions.
2	Child sometimes contributes to class discussions and activities by offering ideas and asking questions.
1	Child rarely contributes to class discussions or activities by offering ideas or asking questions.

Understanding of Concepts Rubric

Level	Understanding of Concepts Descriptor
4	Child shows a thorough understanding of all or almost all concepts and consistently gives appropriate and complete explanations independently. No teacher support is needed.
3	Child shows a good understanding of most concepts and usually gives complete or nearly complete explanations. Infrequent teacher support is needed.
2	Child shows a satisfactory understanding of most concepts and sometimes gives appropriate, but incomplete, explanations. Teacher support is sometimes needed.
1	Child shows little understanding of concepts and rarely gives complete explanations. Intensive teacher support is needed.

Communication of Concepts Rubric

Level	Communication of Concepts Descriptor
4	Child consistently communicates with clarity and precision in written and oral work. Child consistently uses appropriate terminology and vocabulary.
3	Child usually communicates with clarity and precision in written and oral work. Child usually uses appropriate terminology and vocabulary.
2	Child sometimes communicates with clarity and precision in written and oral work. Child sometimes uses appropriate terminology and vocabulary.
1	Child rarely communicates with clarity and precision in written or oral work. Child rarely uses appropriate terminology or vocabulary.

Progress Tracker

Focus ______________________________ **Date** ______________

Name	Class Participation	Understanding of Concepts	Communication of Concepts	Overall Evaluation

Congratulations!

Outdoor Expert

Great Work!

Wildlife Watcher!